A WOMAN'S WARTIME JOURNAL

AN ACCOUNT OF THE PASSAGE OVER A GEORGIA
PLANTATION OF SHERMAN'S ARMY ON THE
MARCH TO THE SEA, AS RECORDED
IN THE DIARY OF

DOLLY SUMNER LUNT

(Mrs. Thomas Burge)

With an Introduction and Notes by
JULIAN STREET

D0920089

CHEROKEE PUBLISHING COMPANY
ATLANTA, GEORGIA
1994

Library of Congress Cataloging-in-Publication Data

Lunt, Dolly Sumner, 1817-1891.
    A Woman's wartime journal : an account of the passage
over a Georgia plantation of Sherman's Army on the march to
the sea / as recorded in the diary of Dolly Sumner Lunt
(Mrs. Thomas Burge) ; with an introduction and notes by
Julian Street.
        p.   cm.
  Originally published: Macon, Ga. : J.W. Burke, 1927.
  ISBN 0-87797-148-X (alk. paper) :
  ISBN 0-87797-149-8 (pbk. : alk. paper) :
    1. Lunt, Dolly Sumner, 1817-1891. 2. United States–History-
-Civil War, 1861-1865–Personal narratives, Confederate.
3. Sherman's March to the Sea–Personal narratives. 4. Georgia-
-History–Civil War, 1861-1865–Personal narratives. 5. Georgia-
-Biography. I. Street, Julian 1879-1947. II. Title
E605.L86 1988   88-20209
973.7'378–dc19   CIP

This book is printed on acid-free paper which conforms to the
American National Standard Z39.48-1984 *Permanence of Paper
for Printed Library Materials.* Paper that conforms to this
standard's requirements for pH, alkaline reserve and freedom
from groundwood is anticipated to last several hundred years
without significant deterioration under normal library use and
storage conditions.

Manufactured in the United States of America

ISBN: 0-87797-148-X
ISBN: 0-87797-149-8 Paper
99 98 97 96 95 94   10 9 8 7 6 5 4 3 2 1

Cover designed by Paulette Lambert

Cherokee Publishing Company
P.O. Box 1730, Marietta, GA 30061

INTRODUCTION

FIRST EDITION

THOUGH Southern rural life has necessarily changed since the Civil War, I doubt that there is in the entire South a place where it has changed less than on the Burge Plantation, near Covington, Georgia. And I do not know in the whole country a place that I should rather see again in springtime—the Georgia springtime, when the air is like a tonic vapor distilled from the earth, from pine trees, tulip trees, Balm-of-Gilead trees (or "bam" trees, as the negroes call them), blossoming Judas trees, Georgia crab-apple, dogwood pink and white, peach blossom, wisteria, sweetshrub, dog violets, pansy violets, Cherokee roses, wild honeysuckle, azalea, and the evanescent green of new treetops, all carried in solution in the sunlight.

It is indicative of the fidelity of the plantation to its old traditions that though more than threescore springs have come and gone since Sherman and his army crossed the red cotton-fields surrounding the plantation house, and though the Burge family name died out, many years ago, with Mrs. Thomas Burge, a portion of whose wartime journal makes up the body of this book, the place continues to be known by her name and her husband's, as it was when they resided there before the Civil War. Some of the negroes mentioned in the journal still live in cabins on the plantation, and almost all the younger generation are the children or grandchildren of Mrs. Burge's former slaves.

Mrs. Burge (Dolly Sumner Lunt) was born September 29, 1817, in Bowdoinham, Maine. That she was brought up in New England, in the heart of the abolitionist movement, and that she was a relative of Charles Sumner, consistent foe of the South, lends peculiar interest to the sentiments on slavery expressed in her journal. As a young woman she moved from Maine to Georgia, where her married sister was already settled. While teaching school in Covington she met Thomas Burge, a plantation-owner and gentleman of the Old South, and presently married him. When some years later Mr. Burge died, Mrs. Burge was left on the plantation with her little daughter, Sarah, (the "Sadai" of the journal) and her slaves, numbering about one hundred. Less than three years after she was widowed the Civil War broke out, and in 1864 this cultivated and charming woman saw Sherman's army pass across her fields on the March to the Sea.

At the time of my visit to the plantation the world was aghast over the German invasion of Belgium, the horrors of which had but recently been fully revealed. What, then, I began to wonder, must life have been in this part of Georgia, when Sherman's men came by? What must it have been to the woman and the little girl living on these acres, in this very house? For though Germany's assault was upon an unoffending neutral state and was impelled by greed and military vanity, whereas Sherman's March through Georgia was an invasion of enemy country for the purpose of "breaking the back" of that enemy and thus terminating the war, nevertheless "military necessity" was the excuse in either case for a campaign of deliberate destruction—which, in the State of Georgia, was measured by Sherman himself at one hundred million dollars.

Therefore when I learned that Mrs. Burge had kept a journal in which were related her experiences throughout this period, I became eager to see it; and I am sure the reader will agree that I did him a good turn when, after perusing the journal, I begged its author's granddaughters—Mrs. M. J. Morehouse, of Evanston, Illinois, and Mrs. Louis

Bolton, of Detroit, Michigan, my hostesses at the plantation—that they permit it to be published.

Their consent having graciously been given, I can only wish that the reader might sit, as I did, perusing the story in the very house, in the very room, in which it was written. I wish he might turn the yellow pages with me, and read for himself of events which seem, somehow, more vivid for the fact that the ink is faded brown with time. And I wish that when the journal tells of "bluecoats coming down the road" the reader might glance up and out through the open window, as I did, and see the very road down which they came.

Imagine yourself in a low, white house, standing in a grove of gigantic oaks surrounded by the cottonfields.

Imagine yourself in a large, comfortable room in this house, in an old rocking chair by the window. From the window you may see the white wellhouse, its roof mottled with the shifting shadows of green boughs above; beyond are the garden and the road, and far away in the red fields, negroes and mules at work. You look down at the large book resting in your lap and read.

JULIAN STREET.

New York, March, 1918

INTRODUCTION

SECOND EDITION

FOR several years this little book has been out of print and those seeking it have been obliged to turn to the shelves of second-hand book stores, where now and then a copy has been found. Meanwhile the demand for the book, though moderate, has been steady, and there have been numerous requests for a reissue.

To the end that this may be accomplished the Century Company, which published the first edition, has kindly relinquished its rights, and the owners of the journal have joined forces with the present publishers in bringing out this new edition as a contribution to the history of the South.

JULIAN STREET.

Princeton, New Jersey,
June, 1927

A WOMAN'S WARTIME
JOURNAL

A WOMAN'S WARTIME
JOURNAL

A NEW year is ushered in, but peace comes not with it. Scarcely a family but has given some of its members to the bloody war that is still decimating our nation. Oh, that its ravages may soon be stopped! Will another year find us among carnage and bloodshed? Shall we be a nation or shall we be annihilated? . . . The prices of everything are very high. Corn seven dollars a bushel, calico ten dollars a yard, salt sixty dollars a hundred, cotton from sixty to eighty cents a pound, everything in like ratio.

JULY 22, 1864.

[*The day of the Battle of Atlanta*]

We have heard the loud booming of cannon all day. Mr. Ward [the overseer]* went over to the burial of Thomas Harwell, whose death I witnessed yesterday. They had but just gone when the Rev. A. Turner, wife, and daughter drove up with their wagons, desiring to rest a while. They went into the ell [a large back room] and lay down, I following them, wishing to enjoy their company. Suddenly I saw the servants running to the palings, and I walked to the door, when I saw such a stampede as I never witnessed before. The road was full of carriages, wagons, men on horseback, all riding at full speed. Judge Floyd stopped, saying: "Mrs. Burge, the Yankees are coming. They have got

---

* Brackets [] in all cases denote comments by the editor.

my family, and here is all I have upon earth. Hide your mules and carriages and whatever valuables you have."

Sadai [Mrs. Burge's nine-year-old daughter] said:

"Oh, Mama, what shall we do?"

"Never mind, Sadai," I said. "They won't hurt you, and you must help me hide my things."

I went to the smoke-house, divided out the meat to the servants, and bid them hide it. Julia [a slave] took a jar of lard and buried it. In the meantime Sadai was taking down and picking up our clothes, which she was giving to the servants to hide in their cabins; silk dresses, challis, muslins, and merinos, linens, and hosiery, all found their way into the chests of the women and under their beds; china and silver were buried underground, and Sadai bid Mary [a slave] hide a bit of soap under some bricks, that mama might have a little left. Then she came to me with a part of a loaf of bread, asking if she had not better put it in her pocket, that we might have something to eat that night. And, verily, we had cause to fear that we might be homeless, for on every side we could see smoke arising from burning buildings and bridges.

Major Ansley, who was wounded in the hip in the battle of Missionary Ridge, and has not recovered, came with his wife, sister, two little ones, and servants. He was traveling in a bed in a small wagon. They had thought to get to Eatonton, but he was so wearied that they stopped with me for the night. I am glad to have them. I shall sleep none tonight. The woods are full of refugees.

JULY 23, 1864.

I have been left in my home all day
with no one but Sadai. Have seen
nothing of the raiders, though this
morning they burned the buildings
around the depot at the Circle [So-
cial Circle, a near-by town]. I have
sat here in the porch nearly all day,
and hailed every one that passed for
news. Just as the sun set here Major
Ansley and family came back. They
heard of the enemy all about and concluded they were as safe here as any-
where. Just before bedtime John, our
boy, came from Covington with word
that the Yankees had left. Wheeler's
men were in Covington and going in
pursuit. We slept sweetly and felt
safe.

*   *   *

SUNDAY, JULY 24, 1864.

No church. Our preacher's horse

stolen by the Yankees. This raid is headed by Guerrard and is for the purpose of destroying our railroads. They cruelly shot a George Daniel and a Mr. Jones of Covington, destroyed a great deal of private property, and took many citizens prisoners.

* * *

JULY 27, 1864.

Major Ansley and family have remained. We are feeling more settled and have begun to bring to light some of the things which we had put away.

* * *

JULY 28, 1864.

I rose early and had the boys plow the turnip-patch. We were just rising from breakfast when Ben Glass rode up with the cry: "The Yankees are coming. Mrs. Burge, hide your mules!" How we were startled and how we hurried the Major to his room! [The Yankees did not come that day, but it was thought best to send Major Ansley away. He left at 2 a. m.]

*   *   *

JULY 29, 1864.

Sleepless nights. The report is that the Yankees have left Covington for Macon, headed by Stoneman, to release prisoners held there. They robbed every house on the road of its provisions, sometimes taking every piece of meat, blankets and wearing apparel, silver and arms of every description. They would take silk dresses and put them under their saddles, and many other things for which they had no use. Is this the way to make us love them and their Union? Let the poor people answer whom they have deprived of every mouthful of meat and of their livestock to make any! Our mills, too, they have burned, destroying an immense amount of property.

* * *

AUGUST 2, 1864.

Just as I got out of bed this morning Aunt Julia [a slave] called me to look down the road and see the soldiers. I peeped through the blinds, and there they were, sure enough, the Yankees —the blue coats!

I was not dressed. The servant women came running in. "Mistress, they are coming! They are coming! They are riding into the lot! There are two coming up the steps!"

I bade Rachel [a slave] fasten my room door and go to the front door and ask them what they wanted. They did not wait for that, but came in and asked why my door was fastened. She told them that the white folks were not up. They said they wanted breakfast, and that quick, too.

"Thug" [short for "Sugar," the nickname of a little girl, Minnie Minerva Glass, now Mrs. Joe Carey Murphy of Charlotte, North Carolina, who had come to pass the night with Sadai] and Sadai, as well as myself, were greatly alarmed. As soon as I could get on my clothing I hastened to the kitchen to hurry up breakfast. Six of them were there talking with my women. They asked about our soldiers and, passing themselves off as Wheeler's men, said:

"Have you seen any of our men go by?"

"Several of Wheeler's men passed

last evening. Who are you?" said I.

"We are a portion of Wheeler's men," said one.

"You look like Yankees," said I.

"Yes," said one, stepping up to me; "we are Yankees. Did you ever see one before?"

"Not for a long time," I replied, "and none such as you." [These men, Mrs. Burge says further, were raiders, Illinois and Kentucky men of German origin. They left after breakfast, taking three of her best mules, but doing no further injury.]

Tonight Captain Smith of an Alabama regiment, and a squad of twenty men, are camped opposite in the field. They have all supped with me, and I shall breakfast with them. We have spent a pleasant evening with music and talk. They have a prisoner

along. I can't help feeling sorry for
him.

*   *   *

AUGUST 5, 1864.

Mr. Ward has been robbed by the
Yankees of his watch, pencil, and
shirt.

*   *   *

NOVEMBER 8, 1864.

Today will probably decide the fate
of the Confederacy. If Lincoln is re-
elected I think our fate is a hard one,
but we are in the hands of a merciful
God, and if He sees that we are in the
wrong, I trust that He will show it un-
to us. I have never felt that slavery
was altogether right, for it is abused
by men, and I have often heard Mr.
Burge say that if he could see that it
was sinful for him to own slaves, if he
felt that it was wrong, he would take

them where he could free them. He
would not sin for his right hand. The
purest and holiest men have owned
them, and I can see nothing in the
scriptures which forbids it. I have
never bought or sold slaves and I have
tried to make life easy and pleasant
to those that have been bequeathed
me by the dead. I have never ceased
to work. Many a Northern house-
keeper has a much easier time than a
Southern matron with her hundred
negroes.

*   *   *

NOVEMBER 12, 1864.

Warped and put in dresses for the
loom. Oh, this blockade gives us work
to do for all hands!

*   *   *

NOVEMBER 15, 1864.

Went up to Covington to-day to pay
the Confederate tax. Did not find the

commissioners. Mid [a slave] drove me with Beck and the buggy. Got home about three o'clock. How very different is Covington from what it used to be! And how little did they, who tore down the old flag and raised the new, realize the results that have ensued!

*   *   *

NOVEMBER 16, 1864.

As I could not obtain in Covington what I went for in the way of dye stuffs, etc., I concluded this morning, in accordance with Mrs. Ward's wish, to go to the Circle. We took Old Dutch and had a pleasant ride as it was a delightful day, but how dreary looks the town! Where formerly all was bustle and business, now naked chimneys and bare walls, for the depot and surroundings were all burned by last summer's raiders. Engaged to sell some bacon and potatoes. Obtained my dye stuffs. Paid seven dollars [Confederate money] a pound for coffee, six dollars an ounce for indigo, twenty dollars for a quire of paper, five dollars for ten cents' worth of flax thread, six dollars for pins, and forty dollars for a bunch of factory thread.

On our way home we met Brother Evans accompanied by John Hinton, who inquired if we had heard that the Yankees were coming. He said that a large force was at Stockbridge, that the Home Guard was called out, and that it was reported that the Yankees were on their way to Savannah. We rode home chatting about it and finally settled it in our minds that it could not be so. Probably a foraging party.

Just before night I walked up to Joe Perry's to know if they had heard anything of the report. He was just starting off to join the company [the Home Guard], being one of them.

* * *

NOVEMBER 17, 1864.

Have been uneasy all day. At night some of the neighbors, who had been to town, called. They said it was a large force moving very slowly. What shall I do? Where go?

* * *

NOVEMBER 18, 1864.

Slept very little last night. Went out doors several times and could see large fires like burning buildings. Am I not in the hands of a merciful God who has promised to take care of the widow and orphan?

Sent off two of my mules in the

night. Mr. Ward and Frank [a slave] took them away and hid them. In the morning took a barrel of salt, which had cost me two hundred dollars, into one of the black women's gardens, put a paper over it, and then on the top of that leached ashes. Fixed it on a board as a leach tub, daubing it with ashes [the old-fashioned way of making lye for soap]. Had some few pieces of meat taken from my smokehouse carried to the Old Place [a distant part of the plantation] and hidden under some fodder. Bade them hide the wagon and gear and then go on plowing. Went to packing up mine and Sadai's clothes. I fear that we shall be homeless.

The boys came back and wished to hide their mules. They say that the Yankees camped at Mr. Gibson's last night and are taking all the stock in the county. Seeing them so eager, I told them to do as they pleased. They took them off, and Elbert [the black coachman] took his forty fattening hogs to the Old Place Swamp and turned them in.

We have done nothing all day—that is, my people have not. I made a pair of pants for Jack [a slave]. Sent Nute [a slave] up to Mrs. Perry's on an errand. On his way back, he said, two Yankees met him and begged him to go with them. They asked if we had livestock, and came up the road as far as Mrs. Laura Perry's. I sat for an hour expecting them, but they must have gone back Oh, how I trust I am safe! Mr. Ward is very much alarmed.

*   *   *

NOVEMBER 19, 1864.

Slept in my clothes last night, as I

heard that the Yankees went to neighbor Montgomery's on Thursday night at one o'clock, searched his house, drank his wine, and took his money and valuables. As we were not disturbed, I walked after breakfast, with Sadai, up to Mr. Joe Perry's, my nearest neighbor, where the Yankees were yesterday. Saw Mrs. Laura [Perry] in the road surrounded by her children, seeming to be looking for some one. She said she was looking for her husband, that old Mrs. Perry had just sent her word that the Yankees went to James Perry's the night before, plundered his house, and drove off all his stock, and that she must drive hers into the old fields. Before we were done talking, up came Joe and Jim Perry from their hiding-place. Jim was very much excited.

Happening to turn and look behind, as we stood there, I saw some blue-coats coming down the hill. Jim immediately raised his gun, swearing he would kill them anyhow.

"No, don't!" said I, and ran home as fast I could, with Sadai.

I could hear them cry, "Halt! Halt!" and their guns went off in quick succession. Oh God, the time of trial has come!

A man passed on his way to Covington. I halloed to him, asking him if he did not know the Yankees were coming.

"No—are they?"

"Yes," said I; "they are not three hundred yards from here."

"Sure enough," said he. "Well, I'll not go. I don't want them to get my horse." And although within hearing of their guns, he would stop and look for them. Blissful ignorance! Not knowing, not hearing, he has not suffered the suspense, the fear, that I have for the past forty-eight hours. I walked to the gate. There they came filing up.

I hastened back to my frightened servants and told them that they had better hide, and then went back to the gate to claim protection and a guard. But like demons they rush in! My yards are full. To my smoke-house, my dairy, pantry, kitchen, and cellar, like famished wolves they come, breaking locks and whatever is in their way. The thousand pounds of meat in my smoke-house is gone in a twinkling, my flour, my meat, my lard, butter, eggs, pickles of various kinds—both in vinegar and brine—

wine, jars, and jugs are all gone. My eighteen fat turkeys, my hens, chickens, and fowls, my young pigs, are shot down in my yard and hunted as if they were rebels themselves. Utterly powerless I ran out and appealed to the guard.

"I cannot help you, Madam; it is orders."

As I stood there, from my lot I saw driven, first, old Dutch, my dear old buggy horse, who has carried my beloved husband so many miles, and who would so quietly wait at the block for him to mount and dismount, and who at last drew him to his grave; then came old Mary, my brood mare, who for years had been too old and stiff for work, with her three-year-old colt, my two-year-old mule, and her last little baby colt. There they go!

There go my mules, my sheep, and, worse than all, my boys [slaves]!

Alas! little did I think while trying to save my house from plunder and fire that they were forcing my boys from home at the point of the bayonet. One, Newton, jumped into bed in his cabin, and declared himself sick. Another crawled under the floor,—a lame boy he was,—but they pulled him out, placed him on a horse, and drove him off. Mid, poor Mid! The last I saw of him, a man had him going around the garden, looking, as I thought, for my sheep, as he was my shepherd. Jack came crying to me, the big tears coursing down his cheeks, saying they were making him go. I said:

"Stay in my room."

But a man followed in, cursing him and threatening to shoot him if he did not go; so poor Jack had to yield.

James Arnold, in trying to escape from a back window, was captured and marched off. Henry, too, was taken; I know not how or when, but probably when he and Bob went after the mules. I had not believed they would force from their homes the poor, doomed negroes, but such has been the fact here, cursing them and saying that "Jeff Davis wanted to put them in his army, but that they should not fight for him, but for the Union." No! Indeed no! They are not friends to the slave. We have never made the poor, cowardly negro fight, and it is strange, passing strange, that the all-powerful Yankee nation with the whole world to back them, their ports open, their armies filled with soldiers from all nations, should at last take the poor negro to help them out against this little Confederacy, which was to have been brought back into the Union in sixty days' time!

My poor boys! My poor boys! What unknown trials are before you! How you have clung to your mistress and assisted her in every way you knew.

Never have I corrected them; a word was sufficient. Never have they known want of any kind. Their parents are with me, and how sadly they lament the loss of their boys. Their cabins are rifled of every valuable, the soldiers swearing that their Sunday clothes were the white people's, and that they never had money to get such things as they had. Poor Frank's chest was broken open, his money and tobacco taken. He has always been a money-making and saving boy; not infrequently has his crop brought him five hundred dollars and more. All of his clothes and Rachel's clothes, which dear Lou gave her before her death and which she had packed away, were stolen from her. Ovens, skillets, coffee-mills, of which we had three, coffee-pots—not one have I left. Sifters all gone!

Seeing that the soldiers could not be restrained, the guard ordered me to have their [the negroes'] remaining possessions brought into my house, which I did, and they all, poor things, huddled together in my room, fearing every moment that the house would be burned.

A Captain Webber from Illinois came into my house. Of him I claimed protection from the vandals who were forcing themselves into my room. He said that he knew my brother Orrington [the late Orrington Lunt, a well-known early settler of Chicago]. At

that name I could not restrain my
feelings, but, bursting into tears, im-
plored him to see my brother and let
him know my destitution. I saw nothing before me but starvation. He
promised to do this, and comforted
me with the assurance that my dwell-
ing-house would not be burned,
though my out-buildings might. Poor
little Sadai went crying to him as to
a friend and told him that they had
taken her doll, Nancy. He begged her
to come and see him, and he would
give her a fine waxen one. [The doll
was found later in the yard of a
neighbor, where a soldier had thrown
it, and was returned to the little girl.
Her children later played with it, and
it is now the plaything of her grand-
daughter.]

He felt for me, and I give him and
several others the character of gentle-

men. I don't believe they would have molested women and children had they had their own way. He seemed surprised that I had not laid away in my house, flour and other provisions. I did not suppose I could secure them there, more than where I usually kept them, for in last summer's raid houses were thoroughly searched. In parting with him, I parted as with a friend.

Sherman himself and a greater portion of his army passed my house that day. All day, as the sad moments rolled on, were they passing not only in front of my house, but from behind; they tore down my garden palings, made a road through my backyard and lot field, driving their stock and riding through, tearing down my fences and desolating my home—wantonly doing it when there was no necessity for it.

Such a day, if I live to the age of
Methuselah, may God spare me from
ever seeing again!

As night drew its sable curtains
around us, the heavens from every
point were lit up with flames from
burning buildings. Dinnerless and
supperless as we were, it was nothing
in comparison with the fear of being
driven out homeless to the dreary
woods. Nothing to eat! I could give
my guard no supper, so he left us. I
appealed to another, asking him if he
had wife, mother, or sister, and how
he should feel were they in my situa-
tion. A colonel from Vermont left me
two men, but they were Dutch, and I
could not understand one word they
said.

My Heavenly Father alone saved
me from the destructive fire. My car-
riage-house had in it eight bales of

cotton, with my carriage, buggy, and harness. On top of the cotton were some carded cotton rolls, a hundred pounds or more. These were thrown out of the blanket in which they were and a large twist of the rolls taken and set on fire, and thrown into the boat of my carriage, which was close up to the cotton bales. Thanks to my God, the cotton only burned over, and then went out. Shall I ever forget the de- liverance?

Tonight, when the greater part of the army had passed, it came up very windy and cold. My room was full, nearly, with the negroes and their bedding. They were afraid to go out, for my women could not step out of the door without an insult from the Yankee soldiers. They lay down on the floor; Sadai got down and under the same cover with Sally, while I

sat up all night, watching every moment for the flames to burst out from
some of my buildings. The two guards
came into my room and laid themselves by my fire for the night.   I
could not close my eyes, but kept
walking to and fro, watching the fires
in the distance and dreading the ap-
proaching day, which, I feared, as
they had not all passed, would be but
a continuation of horrors.

*   *   *

NOVEMBER 20, 1864.

This is the blessed Sabbath, the day
upon which He, who came to bring
peace and good will upon earth, rose
from His tomb and ascended to inter-
cede for us poor fallen creatures. But
how unlike this day to any that have
preceded it in my once quiet home. I
had watched all night, and the dawn
found me watching for the moving

of the soldiery that was encamped about us. Oh, how I dreaded those that were to pass, as I supposed they would straggle and complete the ruin that the others had commenced, for I had been repeatedly told that they would burn everything as they passed.

Some of my women had gathered up a chicken that the soldiers shot yesterday, and they cooked it with some yams for our breakfast, the guard complaining that we gave them no supper. They gave us some coffee, which I had to make in a tea-kettle, as every coffee-pot is taken off. The rear-guard was commanded by Colonel Carlow, who changed our guard, leaving us one soldier while they were passing. They marched directly on, scarcely breaking ranks. Once a bucket of water was called for, but they drank without coming in.

About ten o'clock they had all passed save one, who came in and wanted coffee made, which was done, and he, too, went on. A few minutes elapsed, and two couriers riding rapidly passed back. Then, presently more soldiers came by, and this ended the passing of Sherman's army by my place, leaving me poorer by thirty thousand dollars than I was yesterday morning. And a much stronger Rebel!

After the excitement was a little over, I went up to Mrs. Laura's to sympathize with her, for I had no doubt but that her husband was hanged. She thought so, and we could see no way for his escape. We all took a good cry together. While there, I saw smoke looming up in the direction of my home, and thought surely the fiends had done their work ere they left. I ran as fast as I could, but soon saw that the fire was below my home. It proved to be the gin house [cotton gin] belonging to Colonel Pitts.

My boys have not come home. I fear they cannot get away from the soldiers. Two of my cows came up this morning, but were driven off again by the Yankees.

I feel so thankful that I have not been burned out that I have tried to spend the remainder of the day as the Sabbath ought to be spent. Ate dinner out of the oven in Julia's [the cook's] house, some stew, no bread. She is boiling some corn. My poor servants feel so badly at losing what they have worked for; meat, the hog meat that they love better than anything else, is all gone.

NOVEMBER 21, 1864.

We had the table laid this morning, but no bread or butter or milk. What a prospect for delicacies! My house is a perfect fright. I had brought in Saturday night some thirty bushels of potatoes and ten or fifteen bushels of wheat poured down on the carpet in the ell. Then the few gallons of syrup saved was daubed all about. The backbone of a hog that I had killed on Friday, and which the Yankees did not take when they cleaned out my smoke-house, I found and hid under my bed, and this is all the meat I have.

Major Lee came down this evening, having heard that I was burned out, to proffer me a home. Mr. Dorsett was with him. The army lost some of their beeves in passing. I sent to-day and had some driven into my lot, and then sent to Judge Glass to come over and get some. Had two killed. Some of Wheeler's men came in, and I asked them to shoot the cattle, which they did.

About ten o'clock this morning Mr. Joe Perry [Mrs. Laura's husband] called. I was so glad to see him that I could scarcely forbear embracing him. I could not keep from crying, for I was sure the Yankees had executed him, and I felt so much for his poor wife. The soldiers told me repeatedly Saturday that they had hung him and his brother, James, and George Guise. They had a narrow escape, however, and only got away by knowing the country so much better than the soldiers did. They lay out until this morning. How rejoiced I am for his family! All of his negroes are gone, save one man that had a wife here at my plantation. They are very strong Secesh [Secessionists]. When the army first came along they offered a guard for the house, but Mrs. Laura told them she was guarded by a Higher Power, and did not thank them to do it. She says that she could think of nothing else all day when the army was passing but of the devil and his hosts. She had, however, to call for a guard before night or the soldiers would have taken everything she had.

* * *

NOVEMBER 22, 1864.

After breakfast this morning I went over to my grave-yard to see what had befallen that. To my joy, I found it had not been disturbed. As I stood by my dead, I felt rejoiced that they were at rest. Never have I felt so perfectly reconciled to the death of my husband as I do today, while looking upon the ruin of his lifelong labor. How it would have grieved him to see such destruction! Yes, theirs is the lot to be envied. At rest, rest from care, rest from heartaches, from trouble. . . .

Found one of my large hogs killed just outside the grave-yard.

Walked down to the swamp, looking for the wagon and gear that Henry hid before he was taken off. Found some of my sheep; came home very much wearied, having walked over four miles.

Mr. and Mrs. Rockmore called. Major Lee came down again after some cattle, and while he was here the alarm was given that more Yankees were coming. I was terribly alarmed and packed my trunks with clothing, feeling assured that we should be burned out now. Major Lee swore that he would shoot, which frightened me, for he was intoxicated enough to make him ambitious. He rode off in the direction whence it was said they were coming. Soon after, however, he returned, saying it was a false alarm, that it was some of our own men. Oh, dear! Are we to be always living in fear and dread? Oh, the horrors, the horrors of war!

* * *

NOVEMBER 26, 1864.

A very cold morning. Elbert [the negro coachman] has to go to mill this morning, and I shall go with him, fearing that, if he is alone, my mule may be taken from him, for there are still many straggling soldiers about. Mounted in the little wagon, I went, carrying wheat not only for myself, but for my neighbors. Never did I think I would have to go to mill! Such are the changes that come to us! History tells us of some illustrious examples of this kind. Got home just at night.

Mr. Kennedy stopped all night with us. He has been refugeeing on his way home. Every one we meet gives us painful accounts of the desolation caused by the enemy. Each one has to tell his or her own experience, and fellow-suffering makes us all equal and makes us all feel interested in one another.

*   *   *

DECEMBER 22, 1864.

Tuesday, the nineteenth of the month, I attended Floyd Glass's wedding. She was married in the morning to Lieutenant Doroughty. She expected to have been married the week after the Yankees came, but her groom was not able to get here. Some of the Yankees found out in some way that she was to have been married, and annoyed her considerably by telling her that they had taken her sweetheart prisoner; that when he got off the train at the Circle they took him and, some said, shot him.

The Yankees found Mrs. Glass's china and glassware that she had buried in a box, broke it all up, and then sent her word that she would set no more fine tables. They also got Mrs. Perry's silver.

* * *

DECEMBER 23, 1864.

Just before night Mrs. Robert Rakestraw and Miss Mary drove up to spend the night with me. They had started down into Jasper County, hoping to get back their buggy, having heard that several buggies were left at Mr. Whitfield's by the Yankees.

Nothing new! It is confidently believed that Savannah has been evacuated. I hear nothing from my boys. Poor fellows, how I miss them!

*   *   *

DECEMBER 24, 1864.

This has usually been a very busy day with me, preparing for Christmas not only for my own tables, but for gifts for my servants. Now how changed! No confectionery, cakes, or pies can I have. We are all sad; no loud, jovial laugh from our boys is heard. Christmas Eve, which has ever been gaily celebrated here, which has witnessed the popping of fire-crackers [the Southern custom of celebrating Christmas with fireworks] and the hanging up of stockings, is an occasion now of sadness and gloom. I have nothing even to put in Sadai's stocking, which hangs so invitingly for Santa Claus. How disappointed she will be in the morning, though I have explained to her why he cannot come. Poor children! Why must the innocent suffer with the guilty?

* * *

DECEMBER 25, 1864.

Sadai jumped out of bed very early this morning to feel in her stocking. She could not believe but that there would be something in it. Finding nothing, she crept back into bed, pulled the cover over her face, and I soon heard her sobbing. The little negroes all came in: "Christmas gift, mist'ess! Christmas gift, mist'ess!"

I pulled the cover over my face and was soon mingling my tears with Sadai's.

* * *

[The records in the journal for the year 1865 are full of details of farm work and reflections on the war. For example]:

JANUARY 30, 1865.

As the moon has changed, Julia [the cook] has gone to making soap again. She is a strong believer in the moon, and never undertakes to boil her soap on the wane of the moon. "It won't thicken, mist'ess—see if it does!" She says, too, we must commence gardening this moon. I have felt a strong desire today that my captured boys might come back. Oh, how thankful I should feel to see them once more safe at home!

*   *   *

APRIL 29, 1865.

Boys plowing in old house field. We are needing rain. Everything looks pleasant, but the state of our country is very gloomy. General Lee has sur-

rendered to the victorious Grant.
Well, if it will only hasten the conclu-
sion of this war, I am satisfied. There
has been something very strange in
the whole affair to me, and I can at-
tribute it to nothing but the hand of
Providence, working out some prob-
lem that has not yet been revealed to
us poor, erring mortals. At the begin-
ning of the struggle the minds of men,
their wills, their self-control, seemed
to be all taken from them in a pas-
sionate antagonism to the coming-in
President, Abraham Lincoln.

Our leaders, to whom the people
looked for wisdom, led us into this,
perhaps the greatest error of the age.
"We will not have this man to rule
over us!" was their cry. For years it
has been stirring in the hearts of
Southern politicians that the North
was enriched and built up by Southern

labor and wealth. Men's pockets were always appealed to and appealed to so constantly that an antagonism was excited, which it has been impossible to allay. They did not believe that the North would fight. Said Robert Toombs: "I will drink every drop of blood they will shed." Oh, blinded men! Rivers deep and strong have been shed, and where are we now?— a ruined, subjugated people! What will be our future? is the question which now rests heavily upon the hearts of all.

This has been a month never to be forgotten. Two armies have surrendered. The President of the United States has been assassinated, Richmond evacuated, and Davis, President of the Confederacy, put to grief, to flight. The old flag has been raised again upon Sumter and an armistice accepted.

*　*　*

[May is full of stories of Confederate soldiers, bitterly returning to their homes, and of apprehension of the Yankee troops encamped in the neighborhood.]

*　*　*

MAY 7, 1865.

Sunday evening. Had company every day last week, paroled soldiers returning to their homes. Last night a Mr. and Mrs. Adams, refugees from Alberta, who have been spending the time in Eatonton, called to stay all night. I felt as though I could not take them in. I had purposely kept in the back part of the house all the evening, with my blinds down and door locked, to keep from being troubled by soldiers, and had just gone into my

room with a light, when some one
knocked at the door, and wanted shel-
ter for himself and family. I could
not turn away women and children, so
I took them in. Found them very
pleasant people. They had Govern-
ment wagons along, and he had them
guarded all night. I fear there was
something in them which had been
surrendered, and belonged to the
United States, but he assured me that
with the exception of the mules and
wagon, all belonged to himself. He
said that he left Jeff Davis at Wash-
ington, in this State, on Thursday
morning last. His enemies are in close
pursuit of him, offering a hundred
thousand reward to his captors.

* * *

MAY 14, 1865.

Mr. Knowles, our circuit preacher,
came. I like him. We agree upon a

good many contested topics. He loves
the old flag as well as I and would be
glad to see it floating where it ever
has.

I had a long conversation with my
man Elbert today about freedom, and
told him I was perfectly willing, but
wanted direction. He says the Yankees told Major Lee's servants they
were all free, but they had better re-
main where they were until it was all
settled, as it would be in a month's
time. We heard so many conflicting
rumors we know not what to do, but
are willing to carry out the orders
when we know them.

* * *

MAY 29, 1865.

Dr. Williams, from Social Circle,
came this morning to trade me a
horse. He tells me the people below
are freeing their servants and allow-

ing those to stay with them that will go on with their work and obey as usual. What I shall do with mine is a question that troubles me day and night. It is my last thought at night and the first in the morning. I told them several days ago they were free to do as they liked. But it is my duty to make some provision for them. I thank God that they are freed, and yet what can I do with them? They are old and young, not profitable to hire. What provision can I make?

* * *

[The last two entries of the year 1865, however, supply the journal with the much-to-be-desired happy ending]:

DECEMBER 24, 1865.

It has been many months since I wrote in this journal, and many things of interest have occurred. But above

all I give thanks to God for His good-
ness in preserving my life and so
much of my property for me. My
freedmen have been with me and have
worked for one-sixth of my crop.

This is a very rainy, unpleasant
day. How many poor freedmen are
suffering! Thousands of them must
be exposed to the pitiless rain! Oh,
that everybody would do right, and
there would not be so much suffering
in the world! Sadai and I are all alone
in the house. We have been reading,
talking, and thus spending the hours
until she went to bed, that I might
play Santa Claus. Her stocking hangs
invitingly in the corner. Happy child
and childhood, that can be so easily
made content.!

* * *

DECEMBER 25, 1865.

Sadai woke very early and crept out

of bed to her stocking. Seeing it well filled she soon had a light and eight little negroes around her, gazing upon the treasures. Everything opened that could be divided was shared with them. 'T is the last Christmas, probably, that we shall be together, freedmen! Now you will, I trust, have your own homes, and be joyful under your own vine and fig tree, with none to molest or make afraid.

THE END